EASY PIANO

BOB MARLEY

Photo courtesy Subversive Cinema/Photofest

ISBN 978-1-4803-9525-1

HAL•LEONARD®
CORPORATION
7777 W. BLUEMOUND RD. P.O. BOX 13819 MILWAUKEE, WI 53213

Visit Hal Leonard Online at
www.halleonard.com

CONTENTS

BUFFALO SOLDIER

Words and Music by NOEL WILLIAMS
and BOB MARLEY

Buf - fa - lo sol - dier,   dread - lock Ras - ta;
tak - en from Af - ri - ca,   brought to A - mer - i - ca,

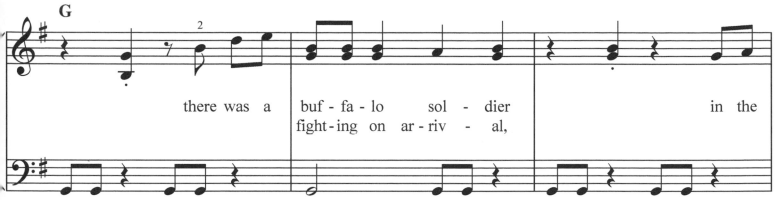

there was a buf - fa - lo sol - dier in the
fight - ing on ar - riv - al,

heart of A - mer - i - ca. Stol - en from Af - ri - ca,
fight - ing for sur - viv - al. Said he was a buf - fa - lo sol - dier,

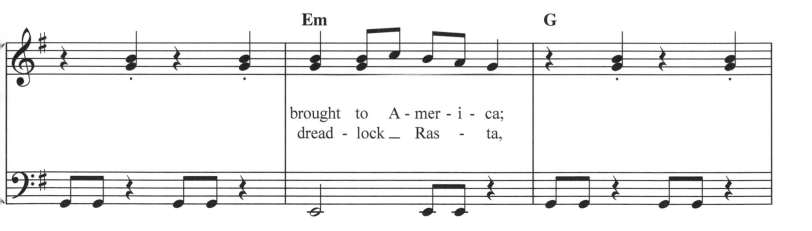

brought to A - mer - i - ca;
dread - lock _ Ras - ta,

fight - ing on ar - riv - al, fight - ing for sur - viv - al.
buf - fa - lo _ sol - dier, in the heart _ of A - mer - i - ca.

6

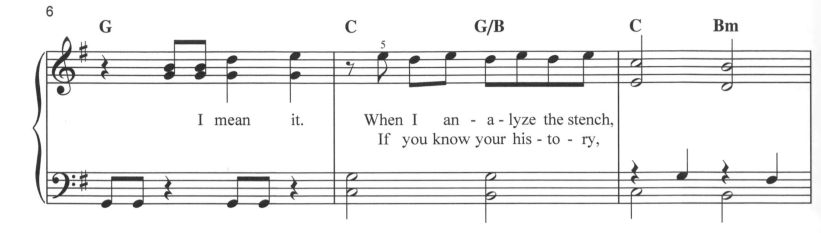

I mean it. When I an - a - lyze the stench,
If you know your his - to - ry,

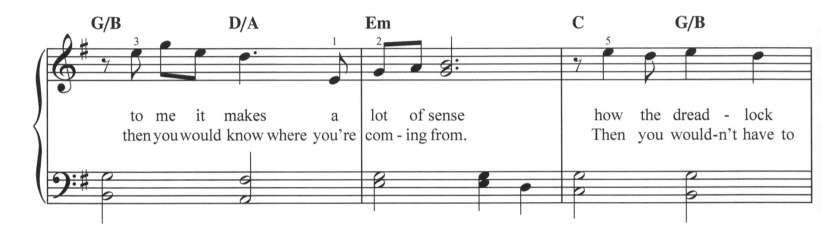

to me it makes a lot of sense
then you would know where you're com - ing from.

how the dread - lock
Then you would-n't have to

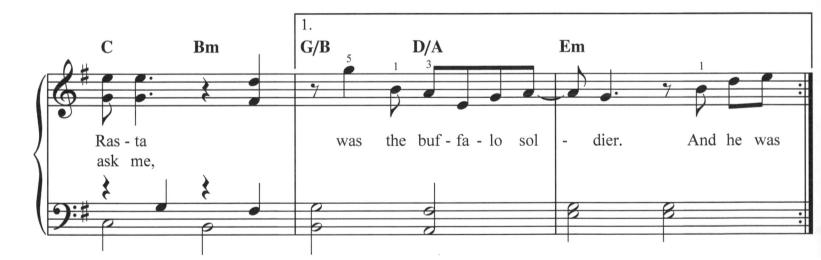

Ras - ta
ask me,

1.

was the buf - fa - lo sol - dier. And he was

2.

who __ the heck do you think I am? I'm just a

buf - fa - lo sol - dier ___ in the heart of A - mer - i - ca,

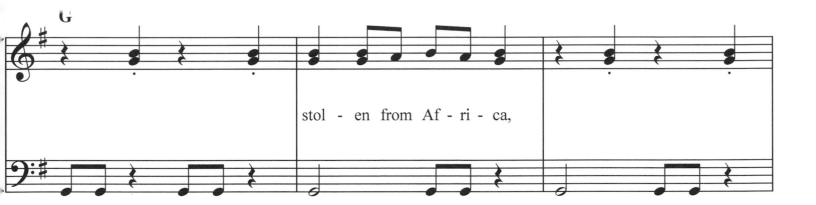

stol - en from Af - ri - ca,

brought to A - mer - i - ca. Said he was fight - ing on ar - riv - al,

fight - ing for sur - viv - al. Said he was a

buf - fa - lo sol - dier _____ in the war for A - mer - i - ca.

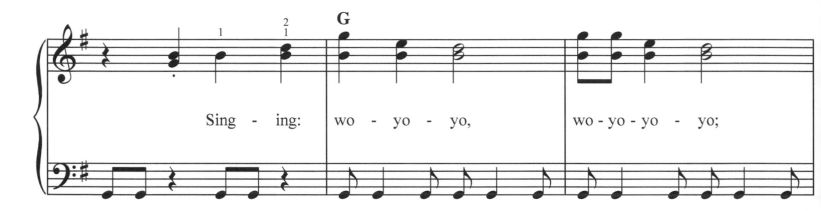

Sing - ing: wo - yo - yo, wo - yo - yo - yo;

wo - yo - yo - yo - yo - yo - yo - yo; wo - yo - yo,

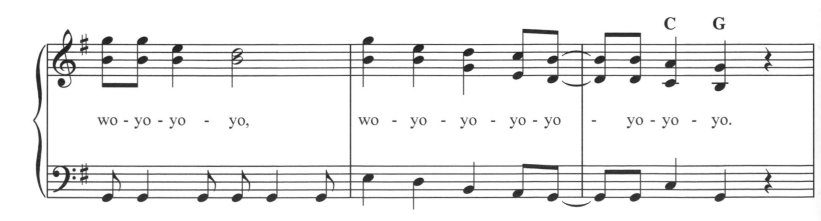

wo - yo - yo - yo, wo - yo - yo - yo - yo - yo - yo - yo.

buf - fa - lo sol - dier,
Trod-ding through Ja - mai - ca, the

dread - lock Ras - ta.
buf - fa - lo sol - dier.

Fight-ing on ar - riv - al,
Fight-ing on ar - riv - al,

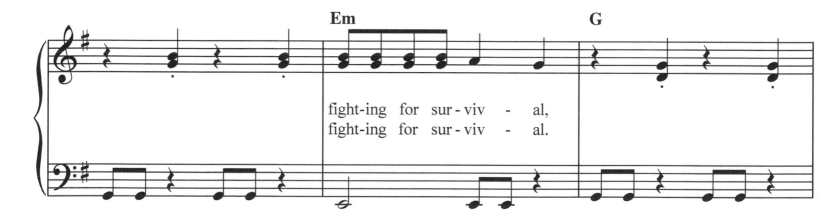

fight-ing for sur - viv - al,
fight-ing for sur - viv - al.

driv - en from the main - land to the heart of the Ca - rib - be - an.
Buf - fa - lo ___ sol - dier, dread - lock ___ Ras - ta.

Sing - ing: wo - yo - yo, wo - yo - yo - yo;

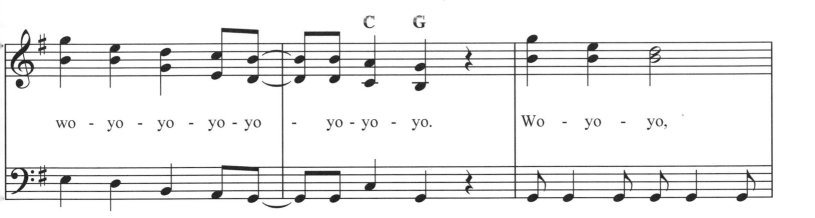

wo - yo - yo - yo - yo - yo - yo - yo. Wo - yo - yo,

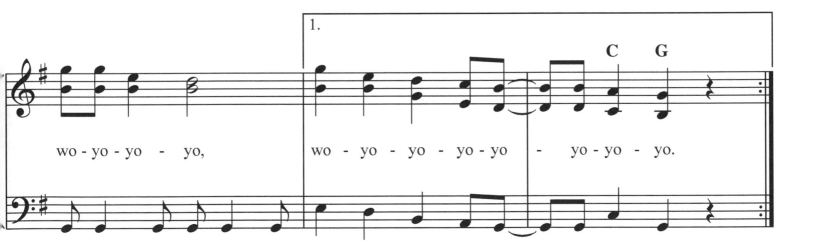

wo - yo - yo - yo, wo - yo - yo - yo - yo - yo - yo - yo.

wo - yo - yo - yo - yo - yo - yo - yo.

COULD YOU BE LOVED

Words and Music by
BOB MARLEY

Moderately bright Reggae

Could you be loved _

and be loved? _

Don't let them   fool you
Don't let them   change you

14

Love _____ would nev - er leave us a - lone.   In the
on - ly, _____   on - ly,   on - ly the

To Coda ⊕

dark - ness there must come out to light.
fit - test of the fit - test shall sur - vive.

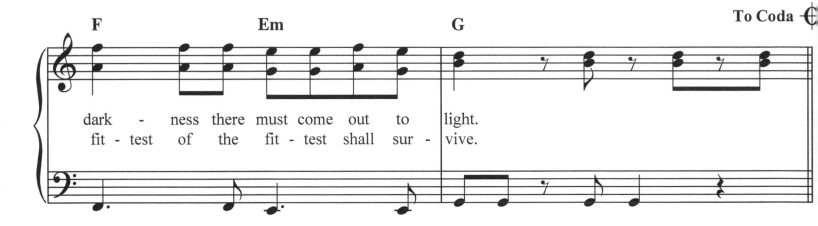

Could you be loved _____

and be loved? _____

Am

The road of life is rock-y and you may stum-ble too. So

while you point your fin - gers, some - one else is judg - in' you.

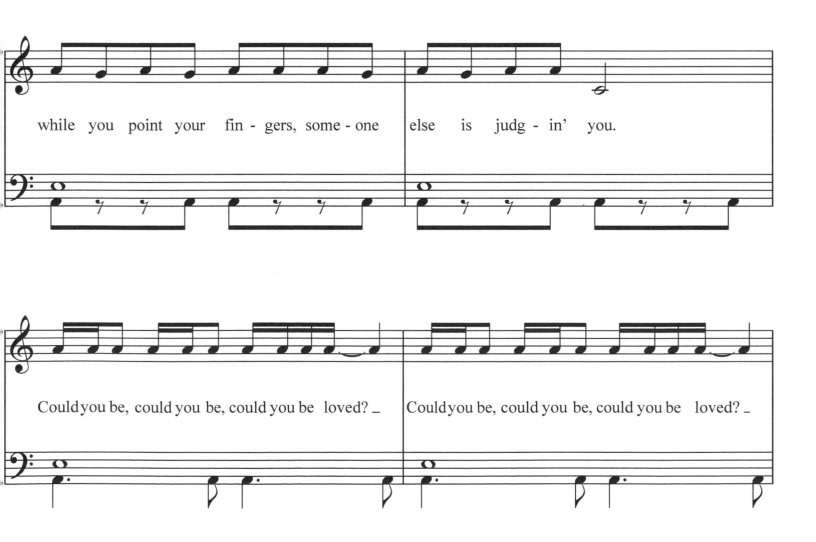

Could you be, could you be, could you be loved? _ Could you be, could you be, could you be loved? _

Could you be, could you be, could you be loved? _   Could you be, could you be, could you be loved? _

CODA

Stay a - live, oh.   Could you be loved _

_   and be loved? _

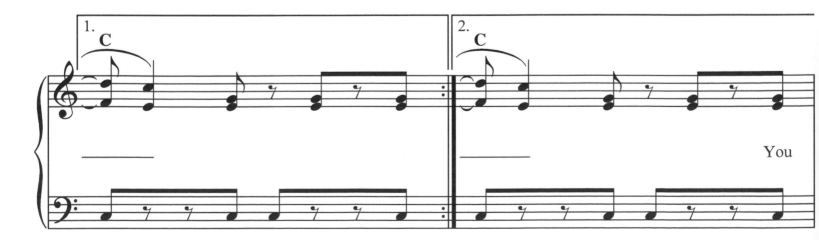

You

GET UP STAND UP

Words and Music by BOB MARLEY
and PETER TOSH

Moderately slow Reggae

1. Get up, stand up,   stand up for ___ your right. ___
2., 3. (*See additional lyrics*)

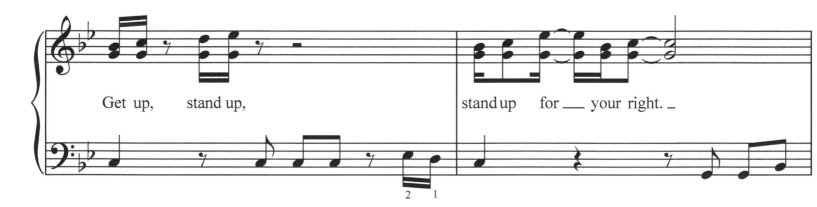

Get up, stand up,   stand up for ___ your right. ___

Get up, stand up,   stand up for ___ your right. ___

stand up for __ your right. __ Get up, stand up,

don't give up __ the fight. __

Additional Lyrics

2. Come on, get up, stand up, stand up for your right.
   Get up, stand up, stand up for the fight.
   Get up, stand up, stand up for your right.
   Get up, stand up, stand up for the fight.

   Most people think great God will come from the sky,
   Take away ev'rything, and make ev'rybody feel high.
   But if you know what life is worth, you would look for yours on earth.
   And now you see the light. You stand up for your right.

3. Yah, get up, stand up, stand up for your right.
   Get up, stand up, stand up for the fight.
   Get up, stand up, stand up for your right.
   Get up, stand up, stand up for the fight.

   We're sick and tired of your ism and skism game.
   Die and go to heaven in Jesus' name, Lord.
   We know when we understand. Almighty God is a living man.
   You can fool some people sometimes,
   But you can't fool all the people all the time.
   So now we see the light. We gonna stand up for our right.

I SHOT THE SHERIFF

Words and Music by
BOB MARLEY

they're try - in' to track me
for what, I don't

down, yeah. They say they want to
know. Ev - 'ry time I

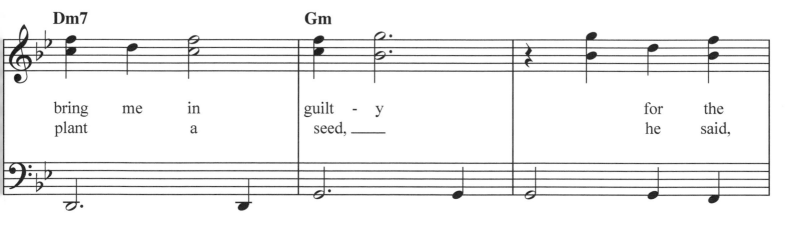

bring me in guilt - y for the
plant a seed, _____ he said,

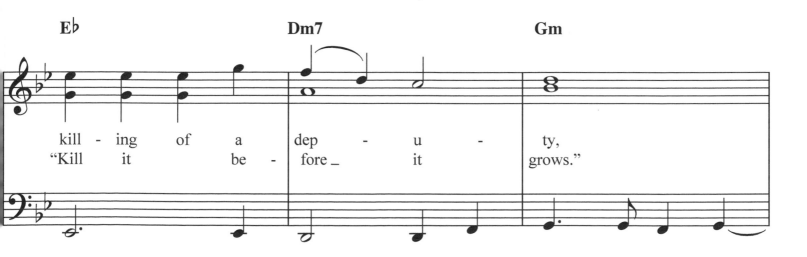

kill - ing of a dep - u - ty,
"Kill it be - fore _ it grows."

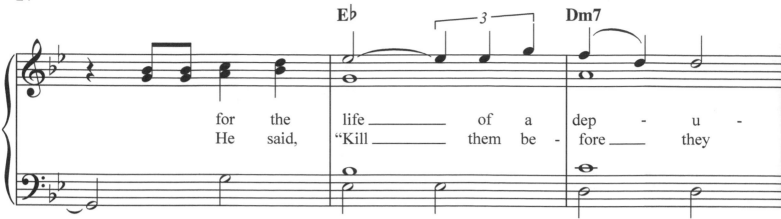

for the   life _____   of a   dep - u -
He said, "Kill _____ them be - fore _____ they

ty. _____   But I say,
grow." _____   And so

oh, _____ now, now.   Oh,
read it in the news.

I   shot   the sher - iff,   but   I
I   shot   the sher - iff,   but   I

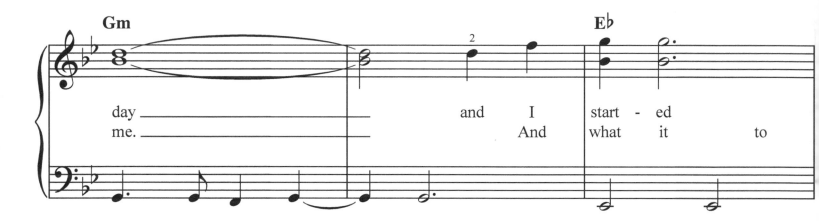

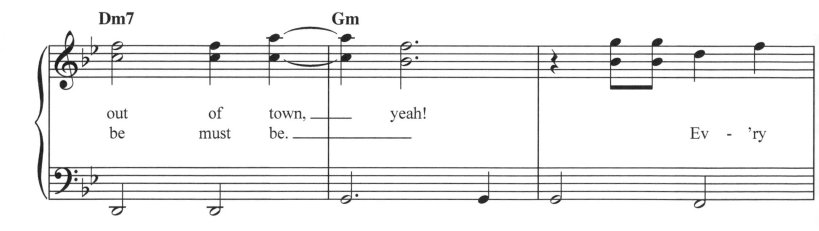

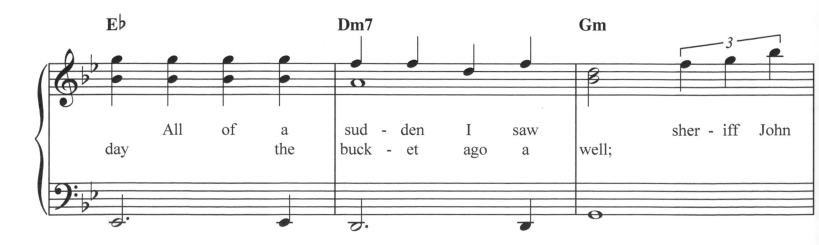

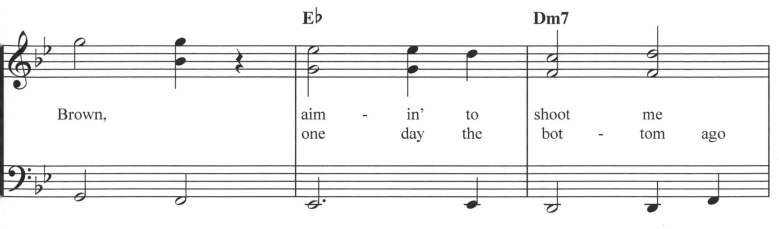

Brown, aim - in' to shoot me
one day the shoot bot - tom ago

down. So I shot, I
drop out. One day the

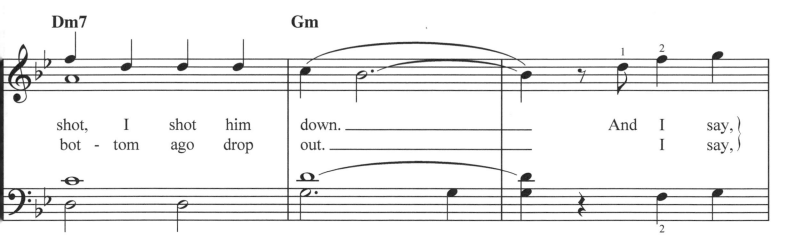

shot, I shot him down. And I say,
bot - tom ago him drop out. I say,

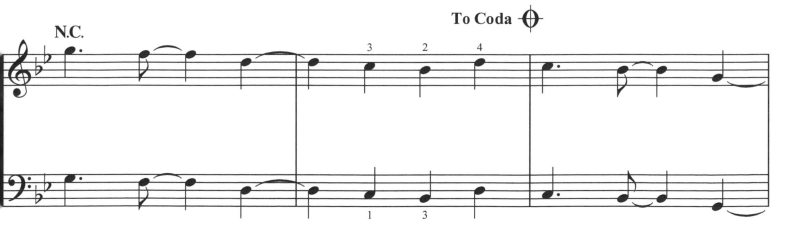

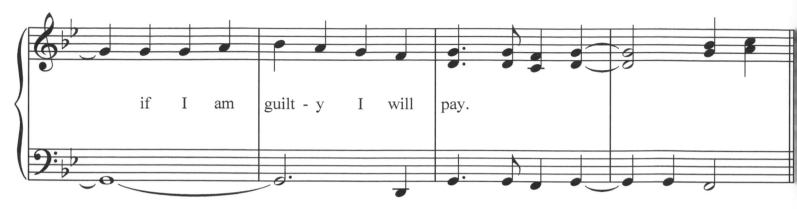

if I am guilt-y I will pay.

I shot the sher - iff, but I say, but I did-n't shoot no

dep - u - ty, oh, no, oh.

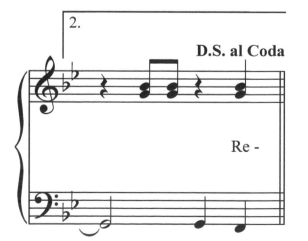

Re -

IS THIS LOVE

Words and Music by
BOB MARLEY

Moderate Reggae

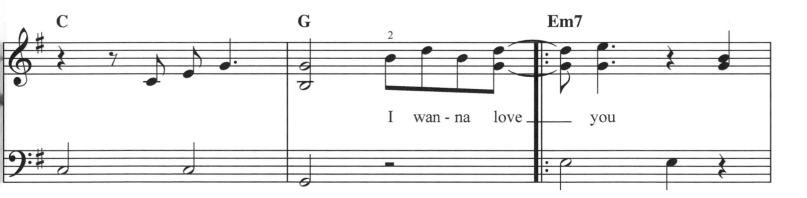

I wan-na love _____ you

and treat you right. _____ I wan-na love _____ you

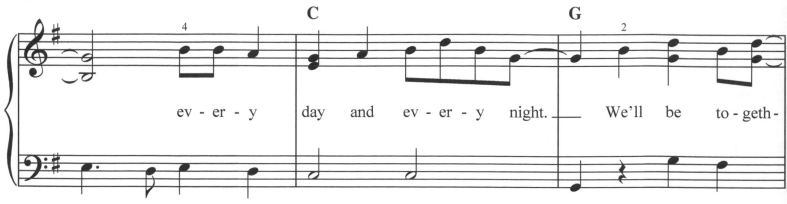

ev - er - y day and ev - er - y night. ___ We'll be to - geth-

- er ___ with a roof right o - ver our heads. ___

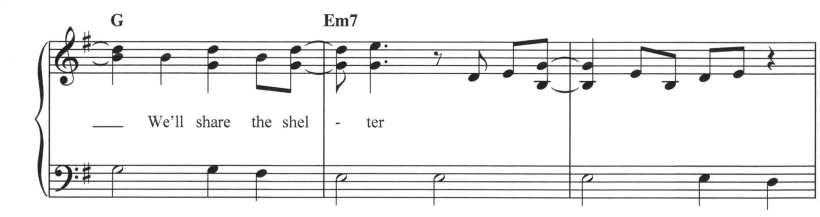

___ We'll share the shel - ter

of my sin - gle bed. ___ We'll share the same ___ room,

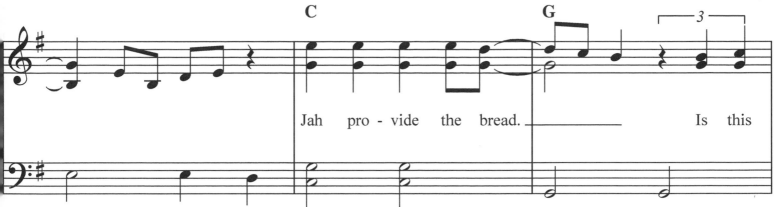

Jah pro - vide the bread. _____ Is this

love, is this love, is this love, is this love that I'm feel - in'? _____

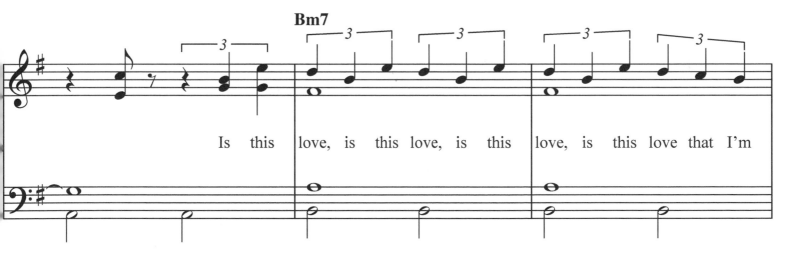

Is this love, is this love, is this love, is this love that I'm

feel - in'? _____

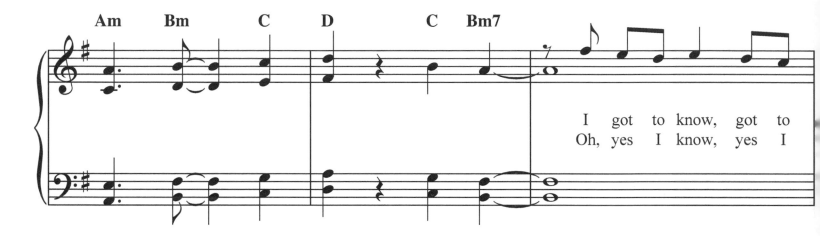

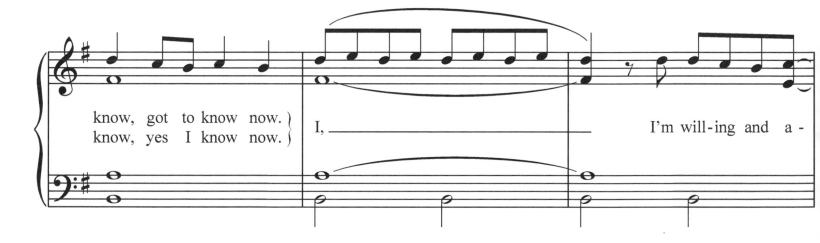

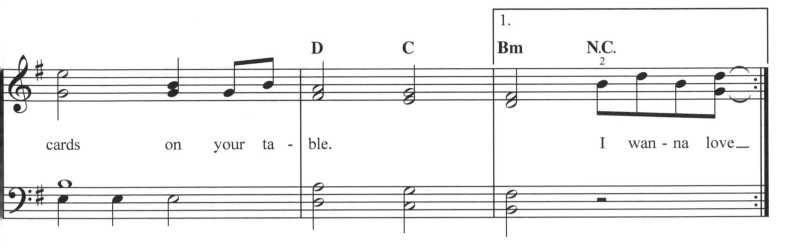

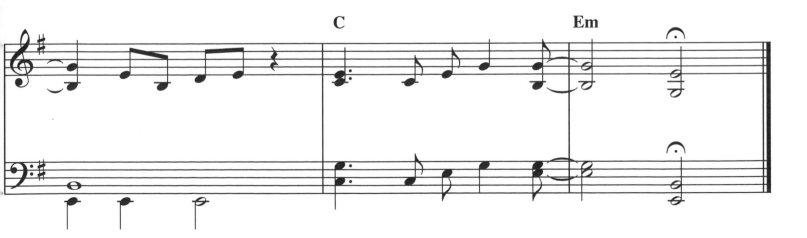

JAMMING

Words and Music by
BOB MARLEY

Ooh, yeah.

Well, al - right. __ 1.We're

jam - min'. __
2., 3. (See additional lyrics)

I wan - na jam it with you. __

We're jam - min', __ jam - min', and I

hope you like jam-min', too. ___   Ain't no   rules, ain't no   vow, ___ we can do

it an - y how. ___   I   and I will see you   through. ___   'Cause ev - er - y

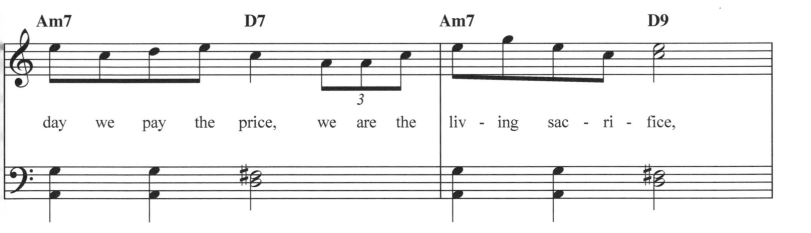

day   we   pay   the   price,   we   are   the   liv - ing   sac - ri - fice,

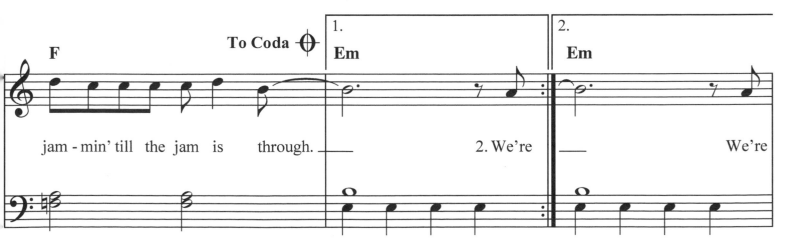

jam - min' till the jam is   through. ___   2. We're   We're

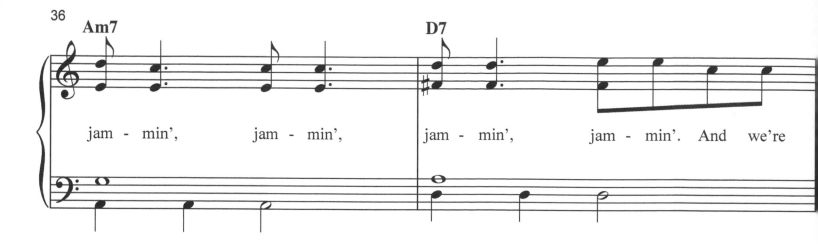

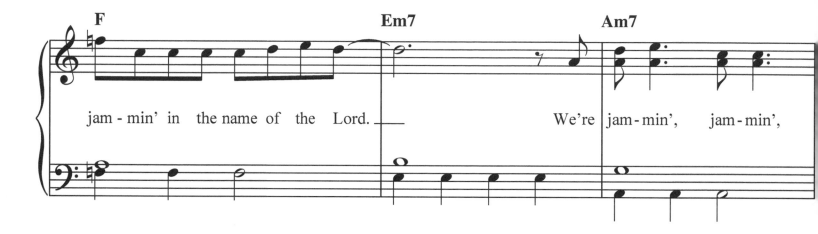

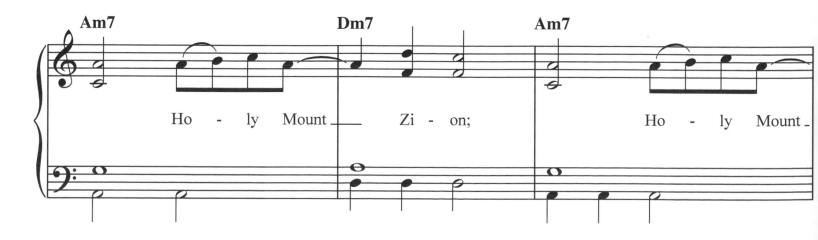

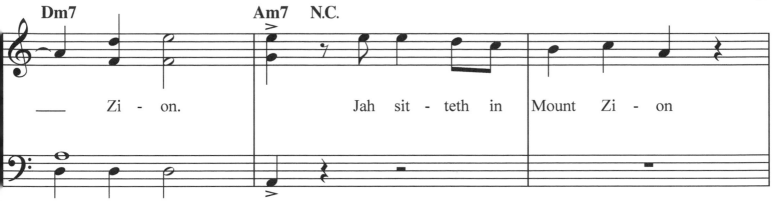

Zi - on. Jah sit - teth in Mount Zi - on

and rules __ all cre - a - tion. Yeah, we're, we're jam - min'.

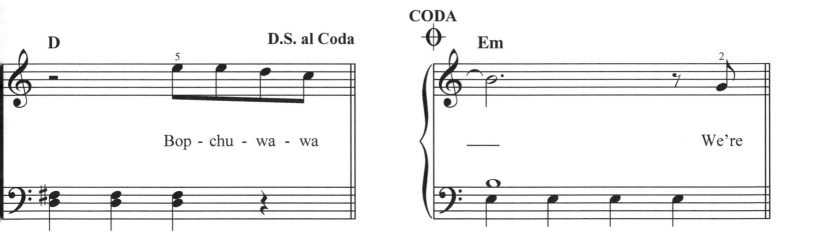

Bop - chu - wa - wa We're

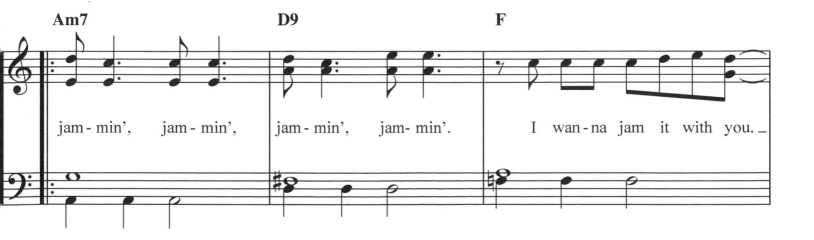

jam - min', jam - min', jam - min', jam - min'. I wan - na jam it with you. __

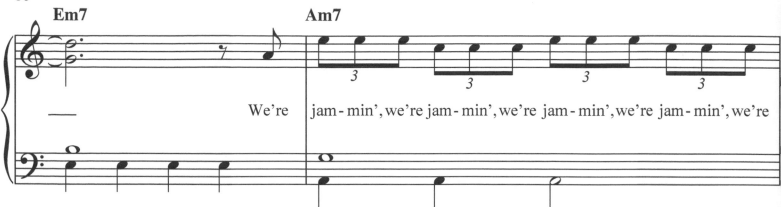

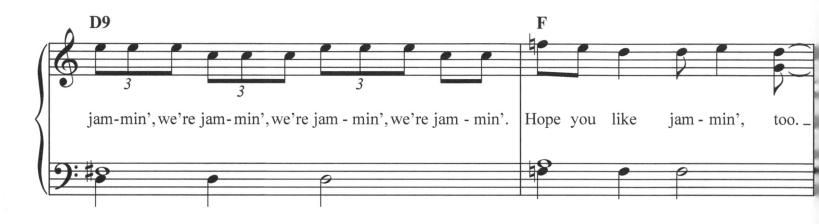

Additional Lyrics

2. We're jammin'. To think that jammin' was a thing of the past.
   We're jammin', and I hope this jam is gonna last.
   No bullet can stop us now, we neither be nor we won't bow.
   Neither can be bought or sold. We all defend the right,
   Jah Jah children must unite, for life is worth much more than gold.

3. We're jammin'. I wanna jam it with you.
   We're jammin', and jam down, hope you're jammin, too.
   Jah knows how much I've tried, the truth cannot hide,
   To keep you satisfied. True love that now exists
   Is the love I can't resist, so jam by my side.

NO WOMAN NO CRY

Words and Music by
VINCENT FORD

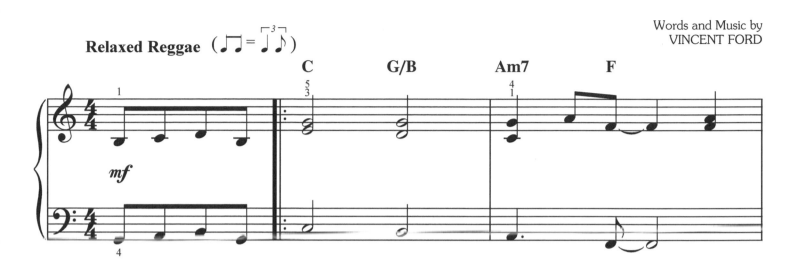

No wom-an, no cry.___

No wom-an, no cry.___

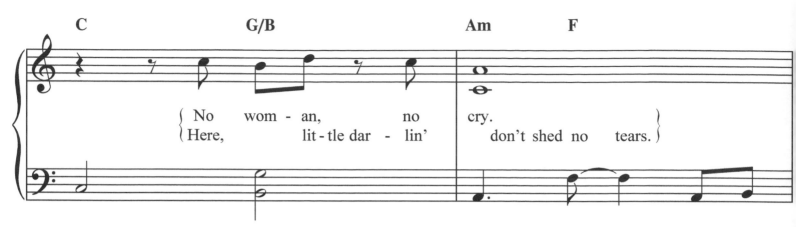

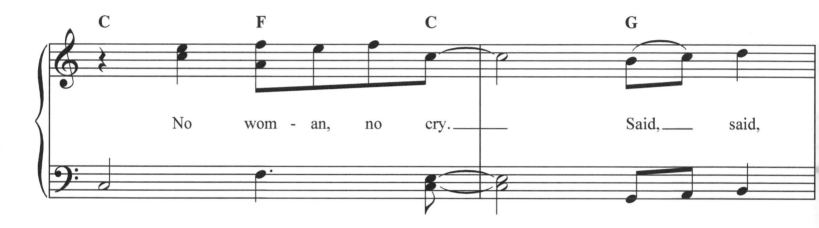

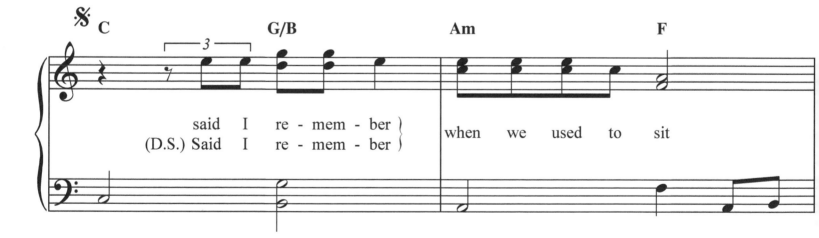

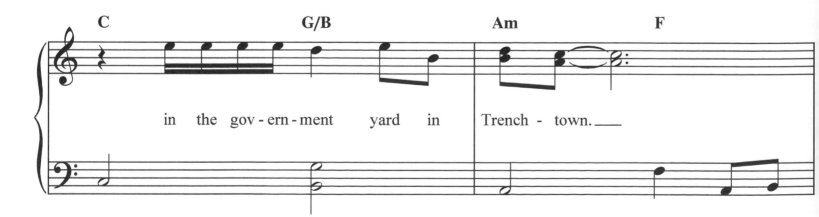

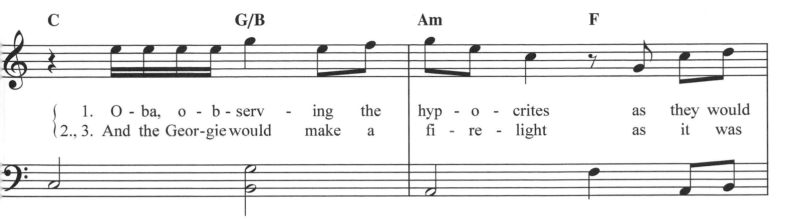

C   G/B   Am   F

1. O - ba, o - b - serv - ing the hyp - o - crites as they would
2., 3. And the Geor-gie would make a fi - re - light as it was

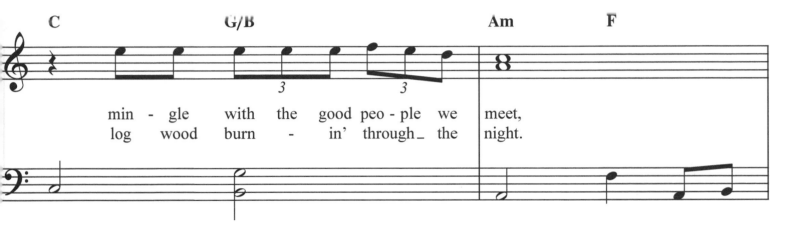

C   G/B   Am   F

min - gle with the good peo - ple we meet,
log wood burn - in' through the night.

C   G/B   Am   F

good friends we had, oh, good friends we've lost
Then we would cook corn - meal por - ridge

C   G/B   Am   F

a - long the way.
of which I'll share with you.

In this bright fu - ture you can't for - get your past,
My feet is my on - ly car - riage, ___

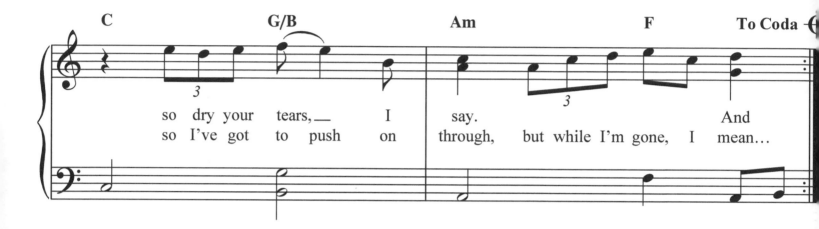

so dry your tears, ___ I say. And
so I've got to push on through, but while I'm gone, I mean...

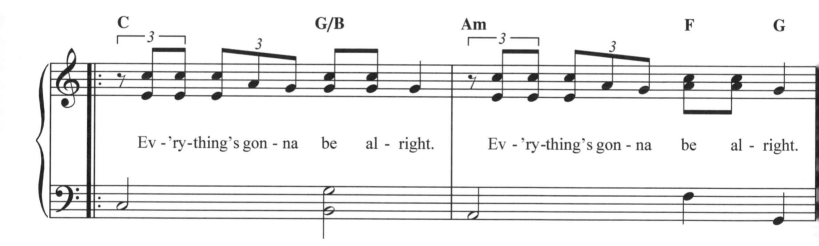

Ev - 'ry-thing's gon - na be al - right. Ev - 'ry-thing's gon - na be al - right.

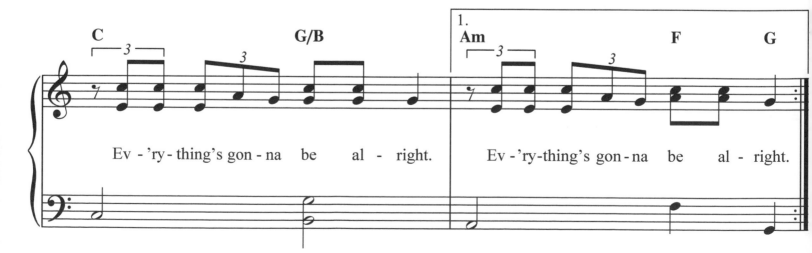

Ev - 'ry-thing's gon - na be al - right. Ev - 'ry-thing's gon - na be al - right.

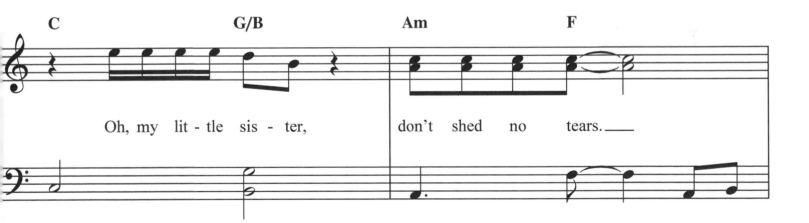

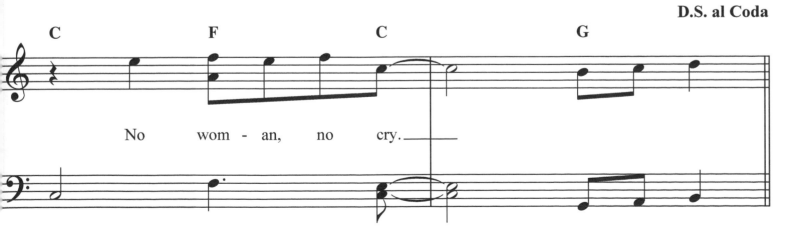

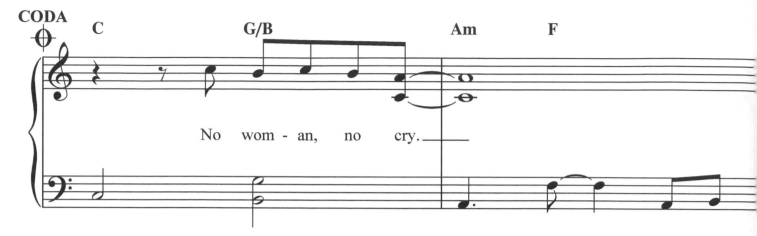

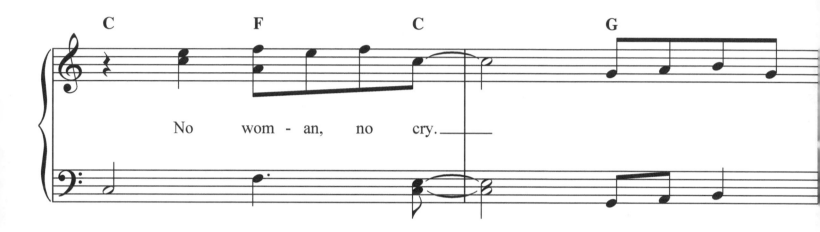

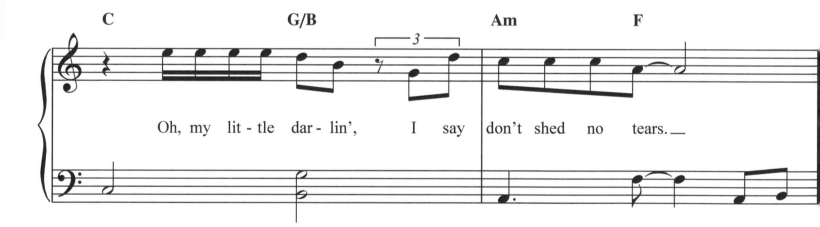

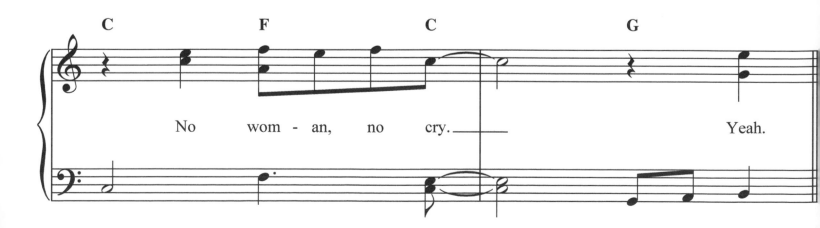

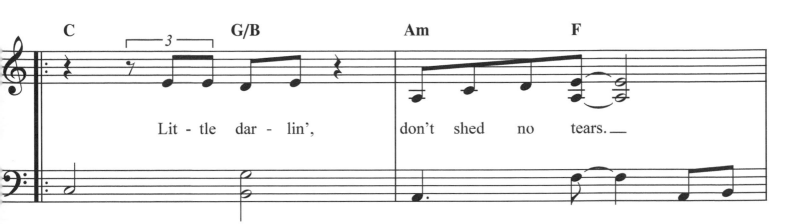

Lit - tle dar - lin', don't shed no tears. __

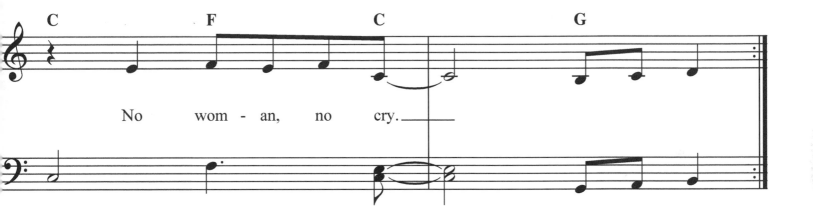

No wom - an, no cry. __

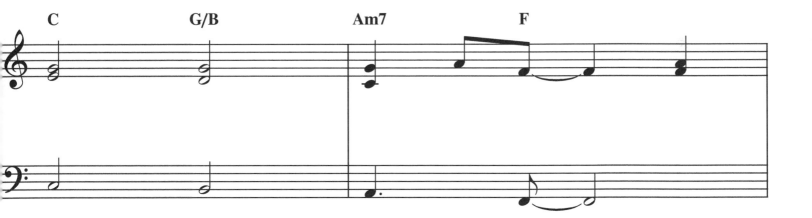

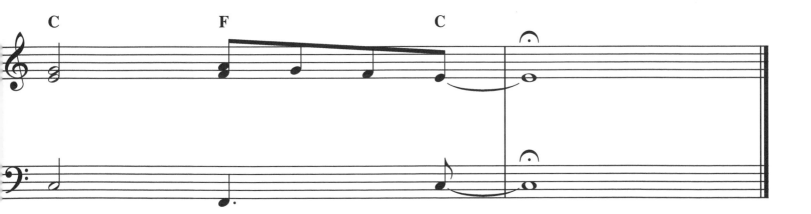

ONE LOVE

Words and Music by
BOB MARLEY

Relaxed Reggae beat

One love, one heart.

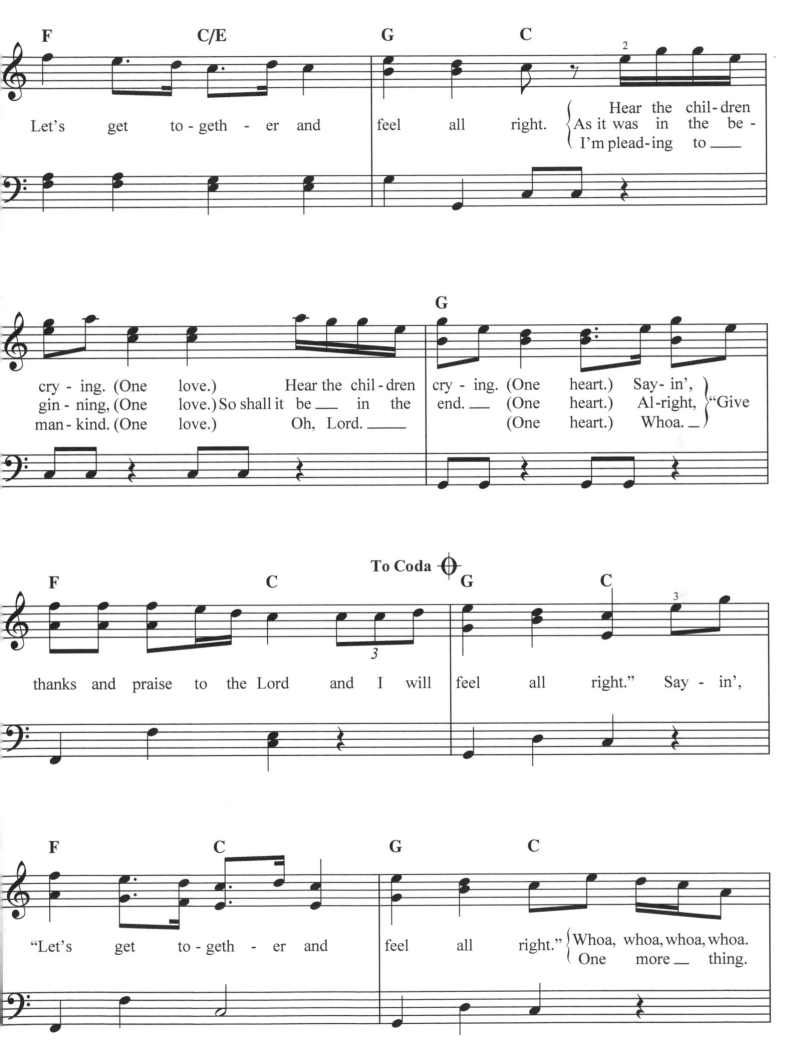

Let them all pass all their dirt - y re - marks. (One
Let's get to - geth - er to fight this Ho - ly Ar - ma - ged-don. (One

love.) There is one ques - tion I'd real - ly love to ask. (One
love.) So when the Man comes there will be no, no doom. (One

heart.) Is there a place ___ for the hope - less sin - ner who has
song.) Have pit - y on those ___ whose chanc - es grow thin - ner. There ain't

hurt all man-kind just to save his own? Be - lieve me.
no hid - ing place from the

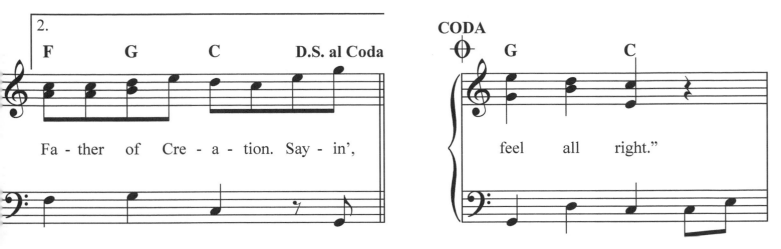

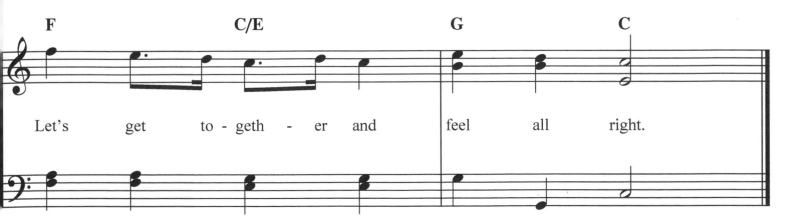

REDEMPTION SONG

Words and Music by
BOB MARLEY

Moderately, Folk style

Old pi - rates, yes, they rob

pate your - selves from men - tal

slav - 'ry, none but our - selves can free our minds. Have no
I. Sold I to the mer - chant ships

min - utes af - ter they took from the bot - tom - less
fear for a - tom - ic en - er - gy, 'cause none of them can stop the time.

pit. But my hand was made strong
How long shall they kill our proph - ets while we

by the hand of the Al - might - y. We
stand a - side and look? Some forward in this gen - er -
say it's just a

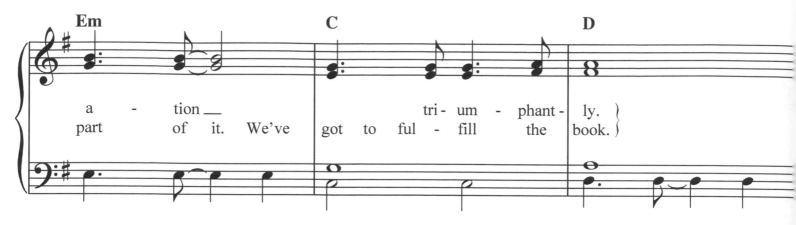

a - tion ___ triumphantly.
part of it. We've got to fulfill the book.

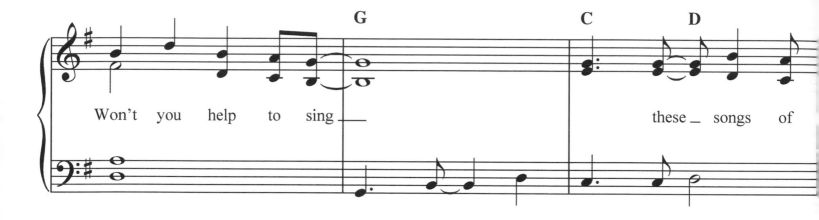

Won't you help to sing ___ these ___ songs of

free - dom? 'Cause all I ev - er had, ___

To Coda ⊕

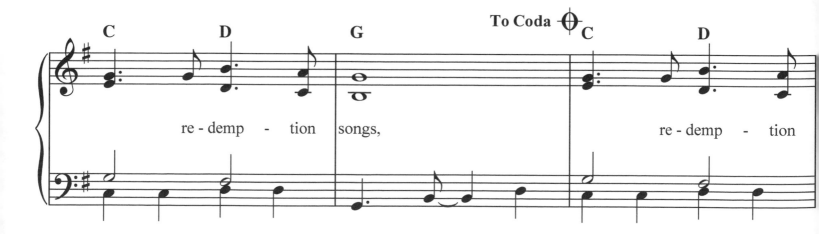

re - demp - tion songs, re - demp - tion

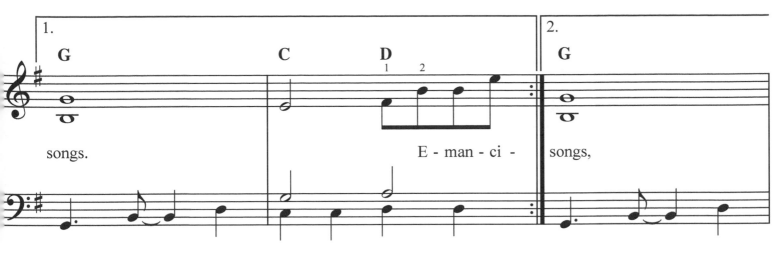

songs.   E - man - ci -   songs,

re - demp - tion songs.

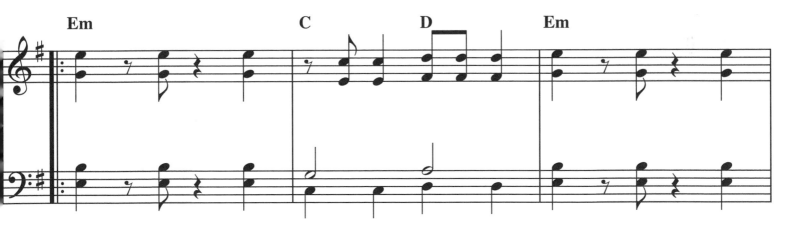

E-man-ci -

all I ev - er had, _

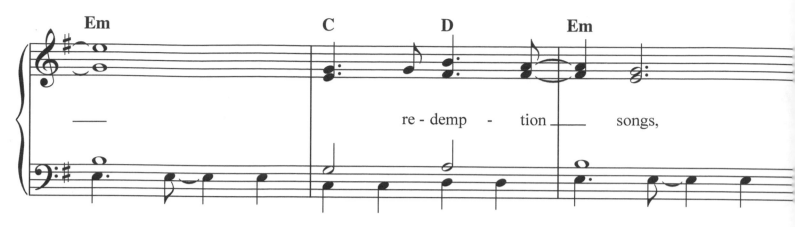

re - demp - tion _ songs,

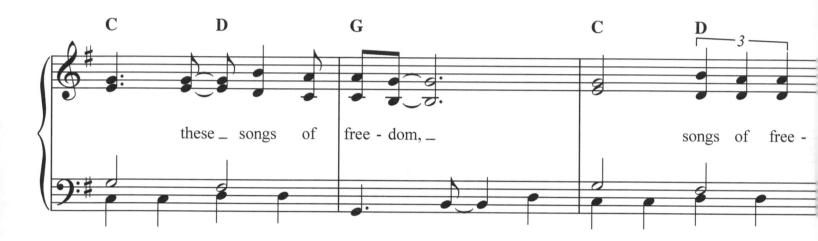

these _ songs   of   free - dom, _   songs   of   free -

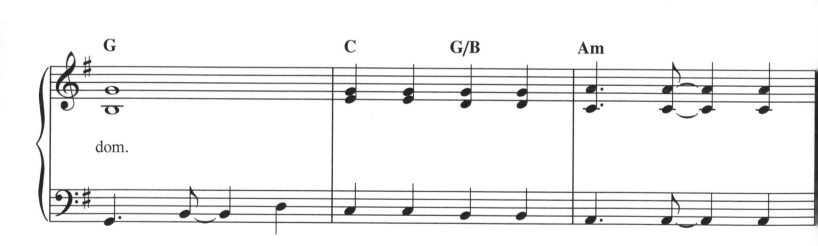

dom.

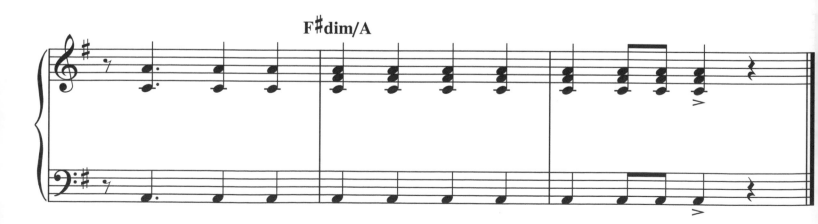

STIR IT UP

Words and Music by
BOB MARLEY

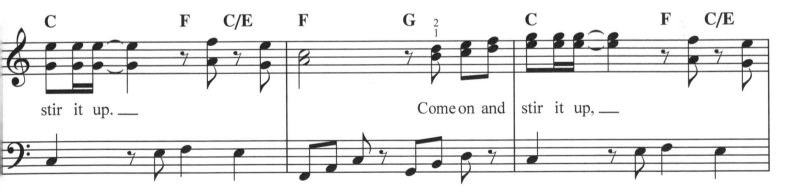

been a long, long time ___ since I've got you on my ___ mind. ___

And now you are ___ here, ___ I say it's so clear. ___

See what we can do, hon-ey, just me and you. Come on and can stir your pot.

Stir it up, ___ lit-tle dar-ling, stir it up. ___

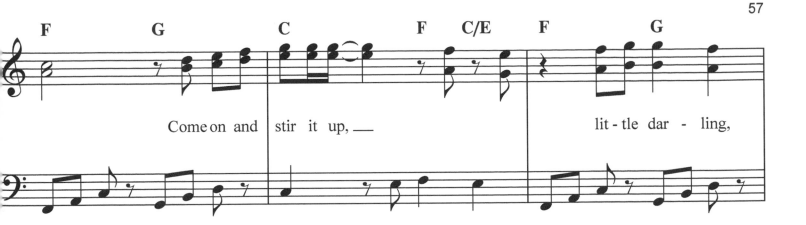

Come on and | stir it up, —   lit - tle dar - ling,

stir it up. —

Additional Lyrics

2. Come on and stir it up, little darling, stir it up.
   Come on and stir it up, little darling, stir it up.
   I'll push the wood, I'll blaze your fire,
   Then I'll satisfy your, your heart's desire.
   Said I'll stir it, yeah, ev'ry minute, yeah.
   All you got to do, honey, is keep it in.

3. And stir it up, little darling, stir it up,
   Come on and stir it up, ooh, little darling, stir it up.
   Oh, will you quench me while I'm thirsty?
   Or would you cool me down when I'm hot?
   Your recipe, darling, is so tasty,
   And you sure can stir your pot.

SATISFY MY SOUL

Words and Music by
BOB MARLEY

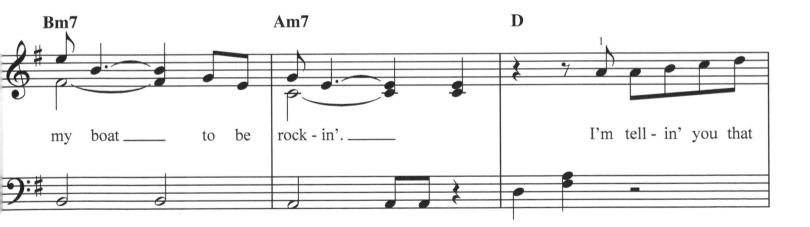

like it, like it like this. So keep it stiff like

this. _____ And you should know, _____

____ you should know by now, _____ I like it, _____

I like it like this. _____ I like it like

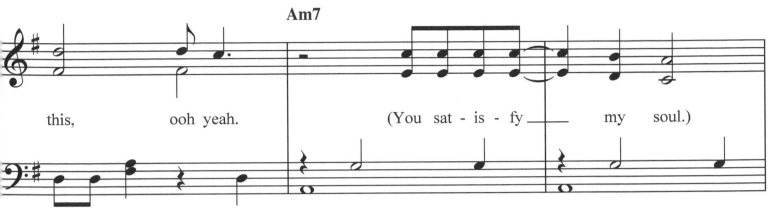

this, ooh yeah. (You sat - is - fy ___ my soul.)

(Sat - is - fy ___ my soul.) (You sat - is - fy ___

___ my soul.) (Sat - is - fy ___ my soul.) Ev - 'ry lit - tle

ac - tion, (You sat - is - fy ___ my soul.) there's a re - ac - tion. (Sat - is - fy ___

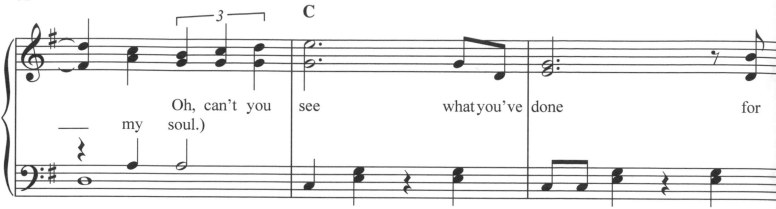

Oh, can't you see   what you've done   for
— my   soul.)

me? _____

I'm   hap - py   in - side

all,   all of the time. _____

When __ we   bend   a   new
D.S. *(See additional lyrics)*

cor - ner, ___

I feel like ___ a,

a sweep - stakes win - ner. ___

When

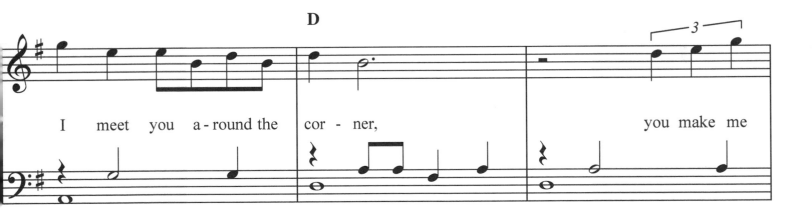

I meet you a - round the cor - ner,

you make me

feel like ___

a sweep - stakes win - ner. ___

Additional Lyrics

When I meet you around the corner,
Oh, I said, "Baby, never let me be alone."
And then you hold me tight,
You make me feel alright.
Yes, when you hold me tight,
You make me feel alright.

SUN IS SHINING

Words and Music by
BOB MARLEY

Sun is shin-ing, the weath-er is sweet.

D.S. *(See additional lyrics)*

Make you want to move your danc-ing feet. To the

res - cue, _____ here I am. Want you to

know, y'all, _____ where I stand.

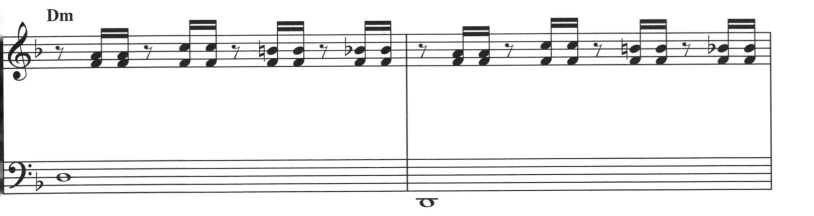

To Coda

Gm7

Mon-day morn - ing, _____ here I am.

Gm7

Tues-day eve - ning; _____ where I stand.

Dm

Wed'n-s'day morn - ing, tell my-self a new day is ris-ing.

Thurs-day eve - ning; get on the rise, a new day is dawn-ing.

Fri - day morn - ing, _____ here I am.

Sat - ur - day eve - ning, _ want you to know, just want you to know just where I ___ stand.

D.S. al Coda

CODA

Gm

We'll lift our heads and give Jah prais - es.

We'll lift our heads and give Jah prais - es, yeah. _____

Sun is shin-ing.

Sun is shin-ing.

Sun is shin-ing.

Sun is shin-ing.

rit.

Additional Lyrics

When the morning gathers the rainbow,
Want you to know I'm a rainbow, too.
So, to the rescue, here I am,
Want you to know just if you can,
Where I stand,
Know, know, know, know, know, know, know, know.

WAITING IN VAIN

Words and Music by
BOB MARLEY

Moderately slow Reggae

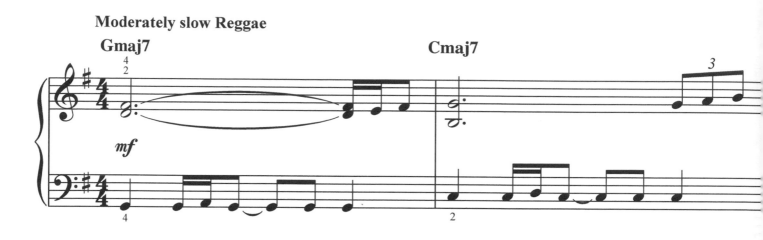

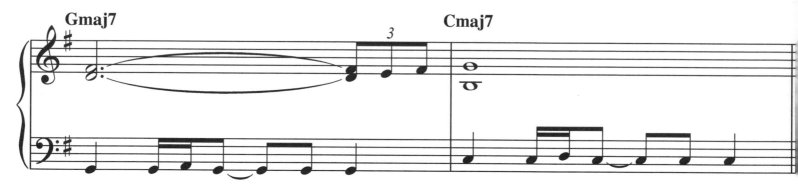

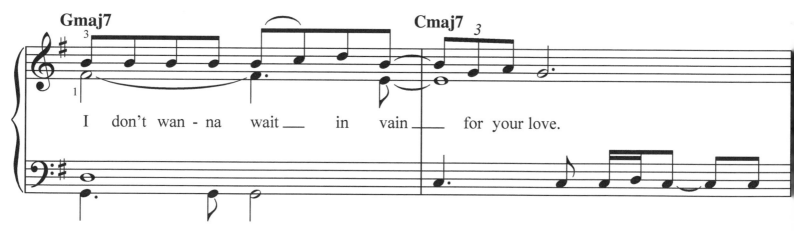

I don't wan-na wait in vain for your love.

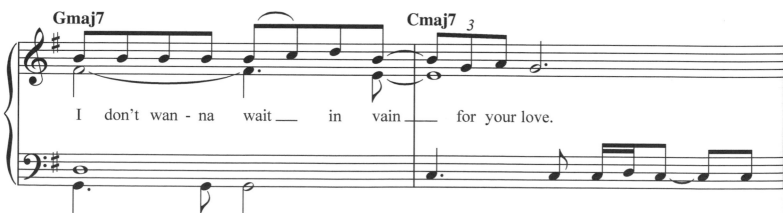

I don't wan-na wait in vain for your love.

From the ver - y first time I blessed my eyes on you, __ girl,
It's been three years since I'm knock - in' on your door, __

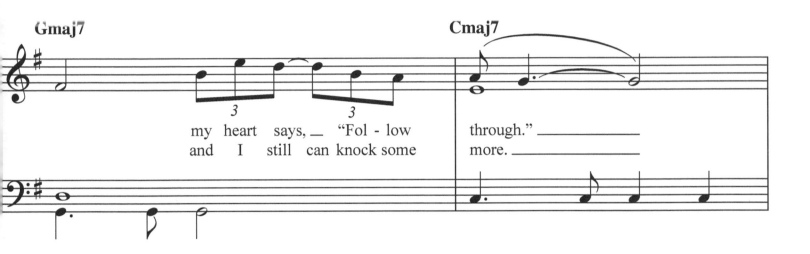

my heart says, __ "Fol - low through." _____
and I still can knock some more. _____

But I know now that I'm way down on your line, __
Ooh girl, ooh __ girl, __ is it feas - i - ble, __ I wan-na know now,

but the wait - ing feel is fine.
for __ I to knock some more?

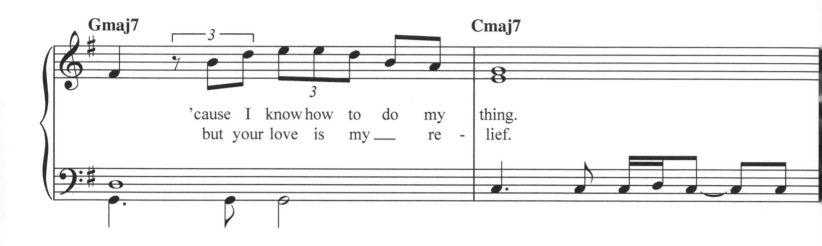

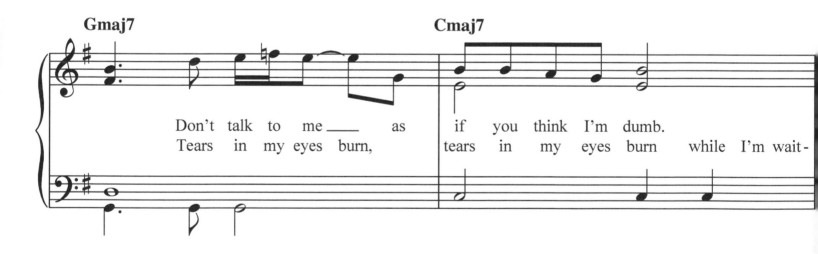

I don't wan - na wait __ in vain __ for your love.

To Coda

I don't wan - na wait __ in vain __ for your love.

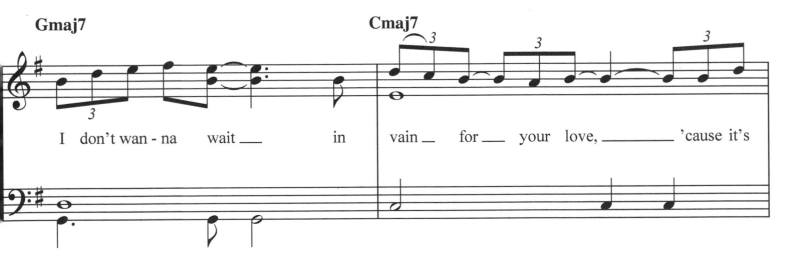

I don't wan - na wait __ in vain __ for __ your love, _____ 'cause it's

sum - mer __ here, I'm still wait - ing __ there. __

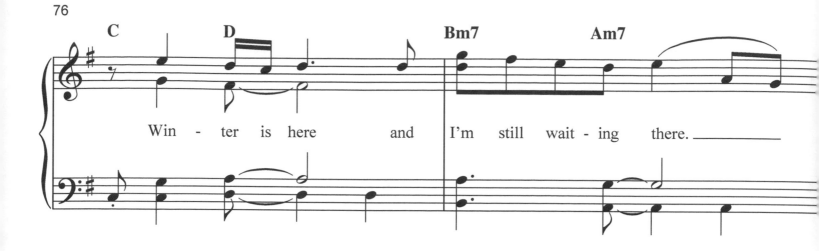

C   **D**   **Bm7**   **Am7**

Win - ter is here   and   I'm still wait - ing there. _____

Gmaj7   **Cmaj7**   **3 Gmaj7**   **3**

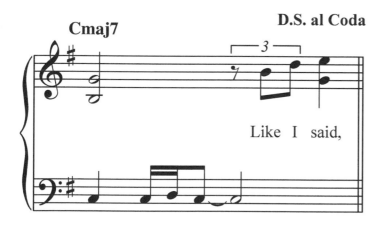

Cmaj7   **D.S. al Coda**

Like I said,

CODA
Gmaj7

I don't wan - na wait __ in vain __

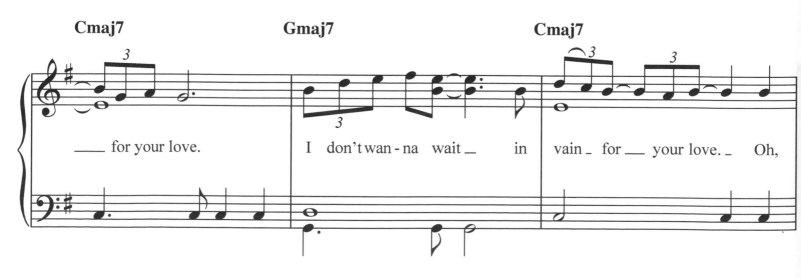

Cmaj7   **Gmaj7**   **Cmaj7**

__ for your love.   I don't wan - na wait __ in vain __ for __ your love. __ Oh,

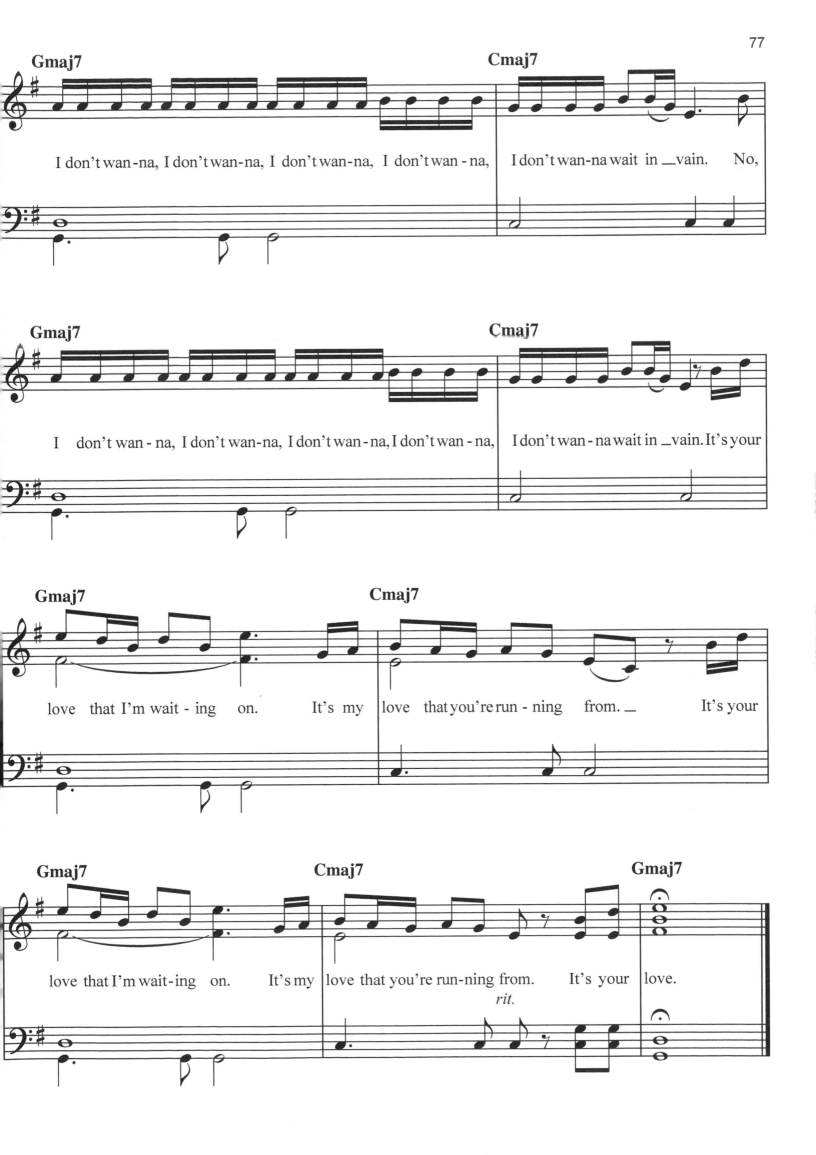

THREE LITTLE BIRDS

Words and Music by
BOB MARLEY

Moderately slow Reggae

Don't

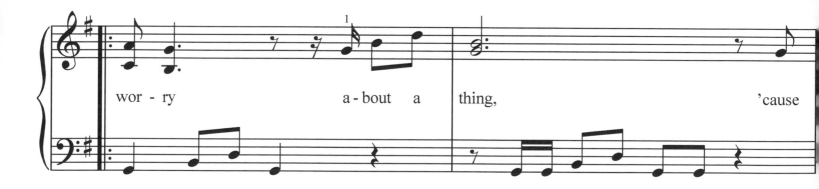

wor - ry   a - bout a   thing,   'cause

ev -'ry lit - tle thing   gon-na be al - right.   Sing - in', don't

wor - ry a - bout a thing, 'cause

ev -'ry lit - tle thing gon-na be al - right. Rise up this

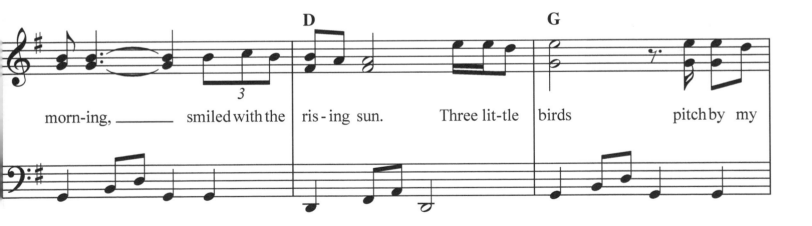

morn-ing, _____ smiled with the ris - ing sun. Three lit-tle birds pitch by my

door-step, _____ sing - in' sweet songs of mel - o - dies pure and true, say - in',